5.99

A Buddhist Life in America

A Buddhist Life in America
Simplicity in the Complex

Joan Halifax

The Wit Lectures
Harvard University
The Divinity School

Introduction by Ronald F. Thiemann

Foreword by Thich Nhat Hanh

PAULIST PRESS
NEW YORK, N.Y. • MAHWAH, N.J.

Cover design by Frank Vitale

Cover illustration by Mary K. Burt

Copyright © 1998 by the President and Fellows of Harvard College

All rights reserved. No part of this book may be reproduced or transmitted in any form or by any means, electronic or mechanical, including photocopying, recording or by any information storage and retrieval system without permission in writing from the publisher.

Library of Congress Cataloging-in-Publication Data

Halifax, Joan.
A Buddhist life in America : simplicity in the complex / Joan Halifax.
p. cm. – (Wit lectures)
ISBN 0-8091-3785-2 (alk. paper)
1. Religious life–Buddhism. 2. Halifax, Joan. 3. Spiritual biography–United States. I. Title. II. Series.
BQ5395.H35 1998
294.3'092–dc21
[B] 97-38781
CIP

Published by Paulist Press
997 Macarthur Boulevard
Mahwah, New Jersey 07430

Printed and bound in the
United States of America

THE WIT LECTURES
Published by Paulist Press

From Brokenness to Community by Jean Vanier
Illuminated Spirit by Govindappa Venkataswamy
Transforming the Mind, Healing the World by
Joseph Goldstein

Foreword

The Wit Lectures at Harvard Divinity School are an exploration of living a spiritual life in the contemporary world, a subject of great importance today as we see the suffering of so many beings in the face of human greed, hatred, and confusion.

This book by Joan Halifax tells us about a life that touches both suffering and joy. It is the story of a Western woman's journey to compassion. It is also a book that explores engaged spirituality, a way of practicing compassionate action in the world.

Joan is an anthropologist and a teacher in the Tiep Hien Order. She has been practicing Buddhism since the 1960s. Her involvement with the civil rights and antiwar movements opened her to issues of social justice that inform her work today. Since 1970, she has worked with dying people and caregivers in order "to inspire a gentle revolution in dying." Joan tells us that her greatest lessons have come from those who are dying. Through her time with dying people, she has seen that fearlessness and freedom are possible.

We know that we must not run away from suffering. If we touch the roots of suffering, we can know how to be free from suffering. Suffering can instruct us. Looking deeply into suffering, we may see the way out of ill-being. The truth of suffering contains the truth of emancipation. The Buddha was a human being made of nonhuman elements. Like a rose that is made of earth, water, air, sunlight, human care, and compost from the garbage, the Buddha was made of his mother and father, his ancestors, his culture. He was also made of suffering as well as joy.

This is true of each of our lives. Each of us contains the freedom of the Buddha. Each of us contains seeds of suffering as well. The Buddha's heart was once broken. Out of his suffering came a true person. Suffering is important. Without suffering, you cannot grow. You cannot realize peace. An organic gardener needs to transform garbage into compost for her roses. We may need to transform suffering into insight, insight into nonduality, insight that leads to compassion. This understanding is at the core of Joan's work and life.

Joan tells us to remove our adornments. Be truth. Go to the Buddha and tell of our suffering. Face our pain with courage and tenderness. Turn also to the world. Turn to it with compassionate action.

—Thich Nhat Hanh

Introduction

In 1995, Joan Halifax, an anthropologist and Buddhist teacher, became the fourth Harold M. Wit Lecturer to visit Harvard Divinity School. Described as "the spiritual successor to Joseph Campbell," she is an accomplished ethnologist. Her rich background in Buddhist practice has for many years played a central role not only in her books, but also in her teaching, research, and fieldwork.

Joan Halifax received a Ph.D. in medical anthropology in 1973 from the Union Graduate School in Cincinnati, Ohio. She has conducted research and taught at Columbia University, the University of Miami School of Medicine, the Maryland Psychiatric Research Center, the New School for Social Research, and the Naropa Institute. She is a Distinguished Visiting Rockefeller Fellow at the California Institute of Integral Studies and president of Upaya, a Buddhist study and retreat center in Santa Fe, New Mexico.

In 1979, she established the Ojai Foundation and School, an international education center in California, where she lived and taught until 1990. Over the years her work has ranged broadly across many themes and disciplines—from health and healing, to ritual life and indigenous peoples, to sacred symbols and religious systems, to environmental and cultural issues, to medical anthropology and psychiatry, to film and photography, to death and dying.

Joan Halifax has been a National Science Foundation Fellow in visual anthropology, an honorary research fellow in medical ethnobotany at Harvard University's Peabody Museum, and a Lindisfarne Fellow. Her books include *The Human Encounter with Death* (with Stanislav Grof), *Shaman: The Wounded Healer,* and *The Fruitful Darkness.* She has also developed the Project on Being with Dying, a national teaching and training program on contemplative work with, and spiritual care of, the dying.

A practicing Buddhist since the late 1960s, Joan Halifax was ordained in 1976 by Dae Soen Sa Nim. In 1990, she received the Lamp Transmission. She is a *dharmacarya* in the Tiep Hien Order of Thich Nhat Hanh.

Harold M. Wit, Harvard College Class of 1949, established the Wit Lectures on Living a Spiritual Life in the Contemporary Age in 1988 to bring to the Harvard community "unusual individuals who radiate in their thought, word and being those spiritual qualities and values that have been so inspiring and encouraging to me along my path. This in the hope that those listening to the lectures and being privileged to be in the good company of such persons might likewise be inspired and encouraged."

Those who know Joan Halifax and her work speak often of the wisdom and the spirit of wonder that suffuse all she says and does. The same was true of the lectures she delivered at Harvard Divinity School. It is my hope that her thoughts on American Buddhism, her insights for leading a spiritual life, and her words about living and dying, comfort and suffering will inspire and encourage readers of this small volume, just as Harold Wit intended.

–Ronald F. Thiemann
Dean and John Lord O'Brian Professor of Divinity
Harvard Divinity School
Cambridge, Massachusetts

"Our own lives are the instrument with which we experiment with truth."—Thich Nhat Hanh

What does it mean to be spiritual in the modern world? It does not mean being a Buddhist, Christian, Muslim, or Jew. Let us look at one person's story to see if there is a partial answer in a life. And perhaps we can consider how a spiritual tradition from Asia has led some of us to a way of being that is closer to home.

Buddhist practice, psychology, and philosophy are touching the lives of many in the Western world. For some of us, Buddhism offers a way of contemplation and seeing that is helping to work with the inheritance of our era. It has touched me for thirty years, first through books, and for more than twenty years through meditation practice.

Of course, I was not born into a Buddhist culture or family. I was born into a Christian family in America at a navy hospital in 1942 during the Second World War. My father was at Dartmouth College learning how to be an officer and a gentleman. History creates the character of a generation; and the qualities of altruism, compassion, and concern for human rights can be found in the lives of many of us who were war babies.

Twenty years after the atomic bomb was dropped on Hiroshima, the sixties exploded in our hearts and minds. Many of us wanted to expand our inner and outer horizons as well as to commit ourselves to human rights and simple living close to the earth. Thirty years later, the nineties seem to be a time when we are renewing our vows and putting them to work in a practical way. This new but old path is called "engaged spirituality," a way for us to bring our spiritual practice into the everyday world.

What follows are fragments of a life that are pieces of a quilt, not a whole cloth. I tell the story to you in the hope that you will see how the inevitable struggles along the way, the passage of time, and a spiritual practice can lead one home. Although this lecture series is about spirituality and everyday life, I hesitate calling myself spiritual. My sense is that the spiritual flows between beings, be they with humans or other beings.

•

A Story

When I was four, a virus infected my eye muscles and I was functionally blind for two years. Children tend to be socialized and to form friendships between the ages of four and six; but because of illness, this did not happen for me in a typical way. I was bedridden much of this time, and the absence of conventional friendships during my childhood was quite significant.

I remember that my life was very internal during my childhood. In the heat and rain of Florida's summers and the cool of its winters, I was sheltered from the natural and social world. I used to lie in my parents' bed listening to my sister and her friends playing outside the window. Because I was not physically normal, I invented a world inside of myself to compensate for loneliness and disability.

During these years of illness, I was cared for by my parents and a black woman named Lilla. Lilla's mother had been a slave, and Lilla herself had no education. Yet to me she was wise and caring. With unending humor, she seemed to love me as if I were her own child. And she seemed to know something about freedom that I needed to understand. My childhood with Lilla was quite typical for many Southerners who looked to the African-American community for care. Many of us were marked and blessed by these kinds of relationships. I started off thinking of her as a servant, only to discover that she was a teacher.

In the 1960s, I went to Harriet Sophie Newcomb College at Tulane University in New Orleans and became involved with the Civil Rights Movement. I could not understand why people like Lilla could not be socially free. I did not understand racism, and eventually I wanted to study anthropology to explore the roots of social injustice and discrimination.

During the early sixties, I was besieged with many questions. What makes people turn in violence against people who are different from them? Why, in a country that values individuality, is difference so deeply discouraged? I thought that learning about culture could teach me something about these questions, and I wanted to work for social justice with people who were outside the mainstream culture. These feelings, I am sure, grew out of my childhood suffering, the strong presence of ethics in the life of my father, the spirit of service in my mother's life, and my relationship with Lilla.

My arrival in New York in 1963 coincided with the escalation of the war in Vietnam and the Civil Rights Movement. During this time, I worked for Alan Lomax, an anthropologist and folklorist who was studying song and movement style cross-culturally. Lomax's politics were to the left; many of his friends had been blacklisted as so-called communists and were prevented from working.

These years with Lomax provided me with more than a taste of social concern and commitment. I was in my early twenties, and it was a fertile time to be in that world of politically and socially motivated people. I also recognized, from my participation in Lomax's cultural research project, that we were not just dealing with social injustice in America, but with the invasion of Western culture into the lives of people everywhere. This acculturation was resulting in the demise or corruption of many cultures and the environments in which they lived.

I wanted to understand something deeper about culture. I realized that it was no longer appropriate for me to sit in a laboratory and work on computer dictionaries analyzing song texts cross-culturally, or to put chrysanthemums in bayoneted guns at the Pentagon. I needed to go into a place that was far away from what was familiar to me. In 1969, after a year of preparation in Paris at the Musée de L'Homme, I drove across the Sahara on my way to live with the Dogon, a people who were in the midst of a rite of passage that marked the death and rebirth of their society.

If I had known what I was getting into, I would never have attempted it. It seemed like such a simple thing—just drive across the Sahara desert. But, in fact, that drive, which took three and a half weeks, had quite an influence on my life. I had never known solitude, and I had never experienced the vastness of landscape that I was to enter. As a child, when I was sick, although the experience was isolating, I still had the benefit of family and Lilla. When I was in school, there was always someone there. When I was working at Columbia University, it was always in relationship with others. But the time in the desert was to mark me, hardening my body and opening my mind. I tasted solitude in the wide expanses of turning sand and sky, and I knew I had come home.

From Gao, a small Saharan town in the heart of Mali, I went down the Niger River on a barge, then drove to Bandiagara to the Dogon people. During my time with the Dogon, I lived close to the earth, walked many miles across hot sand and rock, gazed at clear skies day after day, and looked into the dark faces of people who were kind and patient, working the dry fields for their millet, brewing their heady beer, and readying themselves for the Sigui, a rite of passage that takes place every fifty-three to sixty years.

I had arrived there in the fourth year of the Sigui. An entire culture, not just an individual, was going through a rite of renewal. I looked back at my own culture and saw that we had no authentic rites of passage whereby individuals, families, and the culture could be renewed. What were the consequences, I continually asked myself, of living in a culture where change is not marked?

The Sigui was a time in which the oldest Dogon women, those who were alive during the previous ritual, stepped forward into roles of leadership. It was a time when men, shaved of their hair, were born from the mother-sand of the desert after a night of the whirring of bull roarers. It was a time when men dressed as women, and the world turned into its opposite.

Over the days, watching the Sigui from the shade of sandstone and cliff crevices, I was overwhelmed with the sense of a history that was not bound by time. The history that was unfolding here was born from cosmic or mythic time, and I felt the existential loneliness of a Western woman whose culture's horizon seemed small.

In the midst of these old rites of renewal, I asked

myself: What are the names of my ancestors, my great-grandmothers and fathers? Who were their people? How did they pray? How did they attend to their own suffering and the suffering of others? What did they plant, and what did they hunt? What were the stories they listened to and told by the fire?

•

When I returned from Africa, I was quite ill. During my recovery, I had the good fortune to meet Emanuel Papper, the new dean at the University of Miami School of Medicine. This good friend brought me into the medical school as an anthropologist. I worked there as a "cultural broker" with African Americans and people from the Caribbean and Latin America. As I moved between the hospital and community, I saw that within the co-cultures around the hospital were many individuals who practiced healing. I had the opportunity to be a bridge for some of these healers who made their way into the hospital system.

I also realized that conventional medical training did not seem to be grounded in compassion, although many of the young people who went into medicine were fundamentally motivated by their desire to help others. I asked myself, What does healing mean in our culture? How can compassion and action be brought together? What is the relationship between compassion and equanimity? Can compassion be taught? These and other questions were, fortunately, being addressed at the time by Papper and his colleagues in the medical school. I seemed to have arrived at a good time to bring my sense of concern into action and service.

In 1972, I married Stanislav Grof, a psychiatrist from Czechoslovakia. He was the medical director of a project that gave LSD to people dying of cancer in order to help with their experience of dying. This was a kind of modern rite of passage. When I began this work, I was 30 years old. Although I thought I was somewhat experienced in a medical setting, I was not prepared for the work that I was to do or for the depth of the relationships that would develop between me and those who were dying. All of the people with whom we worked were near death. Most of them were in the extreme of suffering. It seemed that nothing could be done for their pain or fear. They volunteered for this project in hopes of relieving their suffering and having a "gentle death."

In addition to being in very close relationships with dying people, I was also experimenting with LSD myself. I was interested in the nature of my mind, and I also felt that it was unethical to give someone a substance as strong as LSD and not understand something about it oneself. Although I had a meditation practice at that time, it was not strong. I had read about Buddhism and enjoyed meditation, but I had no teacher or community. I lacked any real grounding in meditation practice and had no core of stability. When my ego defenses began to erode from my encounter with LSD, I had no refuge, no place to go. In the middle of this work, I recognized that I needed help and that psychiatry wasn't going to give it to me.

During this experience of mental suffering, which lasted from 1972 to 1978, I had episodes of extreme confusion and anguish. I suffered from full-blown hallucinations and felt deeply identified with the so-called psychotics I had worked with in Florida. I also felt connected with those who were physically suffering and those who were disenfranchised. Being a woman, in a strange way, gave me the permission and latitude to ride straight into a catastrophic mental and physical state. This would have been a rather difficult thing for most men in our culture to go through; but as a woman, not much was expected of me. I felt assigned and resigned to "my fate."

A failed marriage, a failed career, my mind disordered and reputation lost, I went to New York and worked for my friend, mythologist Joseph Campbell, on his book *The Way of the Animal Powers.* Joe was kind and very patient with me. He let me find my way back to sanity through doing research for him on the !Kung, the Mbuti, and other indigenous peoples who used rites of passage as a way to restore order in the heart.

I also realized that I needed help, but Western medicine seemed to offer very little to assuage my suffering.

I sought help in two ways. First, I looked into my own profession to find an explanation for what was going on. The best one I could find was that indigenous cultures have people who go crazy. I thought perhaps I should leave the laboratory and go into the field to spend time with "crazy" indigenous people, medicine people, and shamans who had healed themselves and become healers. Second, I increased my commitment to Buddhist meditation practice.

I went to Mexico several times a year, not to study Huichol Indians, but to study *with* them. I asked for their help. I was very fortunate to meet an old man named Don José Matsuwa. Despite having no right hand and no teeth, Don José was dexterous and sharp in the ways of the mind. With him, through him, and with the help of peyote, my humor was unearthed. I had also seen through eyes older than mine, and I knew I had to find a way to stabilize and integrate what I had seen on the visionary cactus.

At the same time, I took formal refuge in Buddhism. Through my friend Jack Kornfield, I met the Korean teacher Seung Sahn. I asked to be his student and began to practice with him. I sought community, and I sought something I had seen in people who had a steady meditation practice. I wanted to know more about the territories that had been shown to me—suffering and freedom from suffering. In the end, I could not find mental balance, equanimity, or stability using the visionary vegetables. The committed practice of meditation began to foster these mental qualities of strength and openness, and I was, to say the least, relieved.

I must tell you now that Buddhism does not emphasize one's personal story, but rather the practice of the mind studying the mind. The essence of that practice is sitting in stillness and silence and finding the iron pivot in your spine that does not move even in the midst of great suffering.

In my early years of sitting, I tasted that stillness and knew that it was medicine. I had known it as a child and then again in the African desert, but the institutions of Western culture and the nature of my personality had brought me to a qualitative internal and external complexity that overwhelmed me. Concepts about freedom from suffering were helpful, but they were not enough. What I really needed was to become quiet and to look out at the world from the perspective of internal stillness. And although one's personal story may not be so important in Buddhism, one can always use a thorn to remove a thorn.

•

After working for Joseph Campbell, writing a survey of visionary narratives called *Shamanic Voices,* teaching at the New School for Social Research, and traveling to Mexico numerous times, I left New York and went to California to establish the Ojai Foundation, an educational community deeply influenced by Buddhism and the wilderness.

Ojai was an experiment in community where teachers from many cultures and people of many different ages came together to explore what it meant to live a spiritual life. The likes of R. D. Laing, John Lilly, Father Bede Griffiths, Pir Vilayat Khan, Brother David, M. C. Richards, Grace Spotted Eagle, Toni Packer, Thich Nhat Hanh, and others gathered to teach, practice, and consort at Ojai. It was quite complex and rich, and often more than challenging, since the spirit of experimentation was quite strong among the members of our community. As founder and head of Ojai, I encouraged spontaneity and commitment to practice at the same time. This led to a certain intensity and unpredictability that kept surprises happening.

Living in community, as Jean Vanier has suggested, can be an extraordinary experience. Every person in a community carries a piece of who you are. Being in community is a call to being in communion—not to living as if your life does not touch others, but to realizing how deeply our lives intertwine. The experience at Ojai in the late 1970s and 1980s was like this. I lived for eleven years on the earth, without electricity, running water, or plumbing. I lived without a real personal life. This was a life of porosity. The membrane was thin and transparent. King snake and blue jay, red-tailed hawk and wood rat watered at the same ceramic bowl.

Like the wildlife that gathered on the ridge, we humans also watered together. Early each morning the bell called us to meditation. The bell then rang through the day, calling us to meals and meetings. The refuge of practice helped us to look into how we could practice everyday reconciliation. Sitting in council with each other, sharing meditation, working together, and being in the rich flow of teachers and traditions that passed through Ojai seasoned many of us.

It was also difficult for most of us—hot summers, cold and wet winters, a relentless schedule, and minimal shelter. Some nights we would all gather in the kitchen to keep warm. Sometimes the winds blew us apart, scattering our canvas dwellings across the meadows, over ridges, and into the oak forests. In the dry heat of summer, we hid in the shady oaks till dark. In the cold of winter, we took refuge around the campfires and the kitchen stove. The weather was mirrored in our community life.

•

Thây

In the winter of 1985, I met Thich Nhat Hanh (Thây) for the first time at Plum Village in France. For four days, Thây, Sister Chan Khong, Richard Baker Roshi, and I sat and walked together. We enjoyed silent meals of white rice and mustard greens. We walked in fields of early spring jonquils. We talked quietly about what an American Buddhism might look like.

In the old farm house in which we dined, the moments of quiet were so deep that I could hear the inner workings of a wall clock. I had known about Thich Nhat Hanh during the war in Vietnam. I knew his version of peacemaking was different from what most of us were practicing thirty years ago. He had said that "the only way to peace is peace."

In the sixties, we were confrontational and nonviolently violent. We believed we were right and the others wrong. Yet here was a man who could see and feel the suffering on both sides and would not take either. He saw that being spiritual meant helping victims of war and violence, sheltering orphans, and working with governments as well. A spiritual life is not special. It means responding with love and kindness to suffering of every kind.

I realized that what Thich Nhat Hanh had been teaching for many years about meditation in action—serving not just human beings but rivers, mountains, and all creatures—meant that everything can be an experience of practice. Our daily lives are the way we practice meditation; they are the vehicle for awakening, for freeing ourselves and other beings from suffering. When I was younger, I thought that we had to be free from suffering to help others. But Thây's example and teachings made it clear that we can and must do it now.

It seemed strange that I had to go so far from my own root religion to discover one of the important gifts of Western culture and the Judeo-Christian continuum. The tradition of kindness toward others is hardly unique to Buddhism, but I needed to go far from my family's religion in order to discover essential altruism. I also realized that the missing ingredient in my life was the relationship between service and contemplative practice. I had seen them as separate, but I now discovered the treasure of bringing them together.

The Buddha made it clear that suffering is part of existence, but existence is not all suffering. The roots of suffering and ill-being can be traced to the delusion of separateness, the idea that you and I are separate. We may identify with suffering and be fixated on misery; but through practice or other experiences in our lives, we might also see that it is possible to be free from suffering.

In the Fourth Noble Truth, the Buddha addresses the path that leads to the possible liberation from ill-being, characterized by the Threefold Training of Precepts (or the practice of living and nonharming), Concentration, and Wisdom. By working with a practice that helps us to see the world clearly and stabilize our minds, wisdom can arise.

Practicing with Thây and Soen Sa Nim for over twenty years inspired me to reduce the complexity in my own life, to look through the story to the spacious underlying mind ground, and to create a refuge of simplicity for myself and others. This refuge has been the simple practice of meditation.

•

After more than a decade, the "story" of Ojai began to complete itself for me. It was time to leave. I wanted to be free of the institution that had sprung up around me. Like the Handless Maiden in the old folk tale, I needed to separate myself from the familiar and again take time for solitude in order to see where I was and where I was going.

In the seeming intimacy of community life, I had lost my humor. I had lost perspective. I was lonely in the midst of others. I needed functional solitude, a place without history, a place to practice. Ojai did not seem to be a situation where I could lose my identity. On the contrary, my identity was being reified by the circumstances that we were collectively creating.

At the age of 42, eye surgery, a medical accident with radiation, and eye bandages sent me inward. I had to question what was really important in my life. The years ahead unfolded in a pattern of migrations often taking me away from Ojai to the rain forests of southern Mexico and the mountains of Asia.

In 1967, I had hitchhiked across Tibet and circumambulated Mount Kailash, looking for the mountain in my spine. I twice went to Amarnath and Ladakh and once to Annapurna, all in the same year, and found the same big sky everywhere. Could this big mind/big sky, could this mountain be found in the familiar, I asked myself?

Then my mother died. Her death called me again to examine my priorities. If I were to die tomorrow, what would be left undone?

I wanted to be nobody, doing nothing. My departure from Ojai was final. Needing a mountain retreat, I moved to Crestone Mountain Zen Center for a time of quiet, of being in more familiar mountains. Still, I was not ready for *sangha,* for community. Jumping from the pot into the fire, I found myself in another community when what I needed was a hermit's hut. Although I built one above the residential quarters of the Zen center, I still felt the pull of others; and the horizon seemed too small.

Eventually I left Crestone and moved into a hermitage in Abiquiu. At last I had a room of my own. In the oxbow of the Chama River, I found myself settling down. The poet Antonio Machado has written, "In my solitude/I have seen many things/ that were not true." Every day I sat alone on the edge of the brown and churning Chama. In the winter, I watched the bald eagles rest in the arms of bare cottonwoods. In the spring, I witnessed the bosque leaf out and the insects and birds return.

There is great value to be realized in periods of solitude and silence for those whose lives are in and of the world. Although I had gone into solitude for four days every year over the past twenty years, I needed a more sustained period of aloneness to recover the freshness of my spirit and to see that which was not true. "Nowhere to go, nothing to do"—these were the words that informed my days.

After a year, what did I see? It was clear that I wanted to be with people who were dying. I wanted to return to the work that had begun for me in 1970 at the University of Miami School of Medicine. Now I was a bit more seasoned by age and practice, and perhaps I could bring more strength to those who were dying. In being with dying, the true nature of the human mind and heart might be revealed.

•

Being with Dying

In Buddhism, there are archetypes of compassion called *bodhisattvas.* They are awakened beings who have chosen to come back to help liberate those who are suffering. Typically, they have nice clothes, beautiful hair and earrings, and are very pleasant to look at. It is also said that bodhisattvas go in the guise of those who are suffering.

My bodhisattvas have had AIDS, breast cancer, and prostate cancer. They have been brokenhearted, hungry, bereft, and filled with pain. They are the people who have taught me what compassion is really about.

Like Patrick, dying of Kaposi's sarcoma, who said he

felt God had let him live this long so he could take on the suffering of all those men who have KS. Like Jonathan, who lay in perfect equanimity in our midst a week before his death and taught us about acceptance and peace. Like Kenny, who took his own life carefully and peacefully while lying on the earth with friends by his side. Like Joe, whose broken legs take him to bedsides of dying friends.

These beings of perfected intention, who touch us through their suffering, can open within us qualities of compassion, endurance, and stability. They can forge within us, through the experience of relationship, a strength and love that we never thought could be there. These bodhisattvas live under bridges and in the darkest subway tunnels. They are found in prisons, hospital wards, war zones, and mental institutions. We will never know their names, but they know that their identity is not separate from other beings. They are also keenly aware that existence is impermanent, as transient as the lives they live and know.

Some people ask, "Why do you want to be with dying people, where very deep emotions and great physical suffering can arise? Isn't it unbearable?" I feel that we have gravely underestimated the human spirit. We do not see what is possible in each moment of our lives. Like a flower that dies time and time again, we have not accepted the nature of impermanence—that death is inevitable in our lives and as such it invites us to cherish more truly and deeply the present moment. We also do not see that dying is a path to freedom.

I could not see it when I was younger. I anguished over loss. Now I see that we are a culture of grief, so difficult is it for most of us to accept change and loss. But it seems that I have settled down to some degree of equanimity and compassion. I have seen my own mind change, have even lost it. How can I stop the clouds? Would I want to be two years old forever? Even our big old star, the sun, will one day collapse into itself.

Jessica

My niece Dana sent me an amaryllis bulb for Christmas. I planted the bulb in potting soil, put it in the kitchen window, and watered it. Within a short time, a small pale nub pushed out of the top of the bulb, developed a point, and began to turn green. In quite a short time, the stalk was tall with four buds off its strong vertical shaft.

My travel schedule took me out of town. When I returned in the evening a week later, I came through the kitchen door and saw the amaryllis. It was extraordinarily beautiful, glistening in the kitchen light. Four pink and white flowers flared out in the four directions. I put my hands together and bowed. It was one of the most beautiful beings I had ever seen. I was happy because I felt the presence of my beloved niece in her.

After a week, the edges of the flowers became brown; and in a few more days, the flowers had all wilted. One morning I took a pair of pruning scissors, bowed, held the withered stalk, and delicately cut it off at the bulb. I put the wrinkled stalk and faded brown flowers into the compost pile. Within ten days, another stalk came up and four more flowers bloomed. Again it went through its cycle of radiance and then dying, and once more I cut the stalk at the root of the bulb.

While the amaryllis flower was going through its changes, a young woman named Jessica came into my life. Jessica had been diagnosed the previous June with breast cancer. Her cancer was quite aggressive and had metastasized into her liver, lungs, and brain. In spite of her condition, Jessica had a spirit that would not quit.

Shortly after we met, fifteen women who either had breast cancer or were survivors of breast cancer came to spend the day doing meditation with me. Because Jessica's disease was so advanced, her presence seemed to be unsettling for some of the women who were survivors. At the end of the retreat, we tried to listen to each person as if it were her last day on earth. We tried to hear from the depths of our hearts, knowing how fragile our connection to life is. Sitting in a circle, we spoke one after another as openly and honestly as we were able. This practice is called "council" and has its roots in the Quaker and Native American traditions.

When it was Jessica's turn to speak, she received the Zen stick and took it with both hands. The woman who offered it to her used both of her hands to pass it on to Jessica. Jessica held the stick in silence and then said slowly, "I wish I could accept my death the way I accept this stick." She then handed it back to the woman and said, "Please let me accept the stick again."

Several weeks later, Jessica was sitting in council with us. One of the women in the group, Margrit, a nurse, expressed great hopelessness and helplessness at not being able to bring love and compassion into a conventional hospital setting. Jessica spoke after her. She looked like a Zen nun—no hair, dressed in black, her ears transparent. She also had radiation burns on her neck, she was very thin, and her face had a pale yellow cast to it. In spite of her physical delicacy, she made it clear that her problem was not self-pity. People seemed to change their minds in her presence. We knew that Jessica was close to death; we also felt that she was closer to life than most of us.

One day Jessica asked me to come over. I lay down in bed beside her, and we held hands without talking. Later she said, "Joan, would you mind telling me how to die?"

"Jessica," I replied, "I don't know how to die. I am learning from you."

"Tell me what you know," she insisted.

I said quietly, "Let's just breathe together and enjoy each other." So we breathed. Because her out-breath was very ragged, I suggested, "When you breathe, let your attention be on your out-breath, because that will be the last breath, indeed, this out-breath. When you let go of that out-breath, let go into joy. Maybe you will inhale, maybe not." We worked with that and then with the *gatha* [Zen verse]: "In, out, deep, slow, calm, ease, smile, release, present moment, only moment."

About an hour later, Jessica asked me about the *bardos,* the stages of life and death that are described by Tibetan Buddhists. Although I told her about them, I said, "Just keep it really simple. Don't get busy with your dying, get simple with it. Be spacious with it."

That was Wednesday. On Saturday her grave was dug, and on Monday she was admitted into the same hospital where Margrit worked. On Tuesday morning, Margrit, the woman who had felt so hopeless the week before, came onto Jessica's floor as the nurse. She walked into Room 201 not knowing that the patient in that room was Jessica. Seeing her, Margrit asked her family and friends if a nonresuscitation order had been signed. Jessica and her caregivers did not know what that was, so Margrit explained that it was an order not to resuscitate once a person has died.

The order was signed. There would be no attempt to resuscitate Jessica at the time of her death. At ten of twelve, Jessica said, "I'm dying." In thirty minutes, she was gone. She died in the presence of family and friends. Near the end, she said she was afraid, and she was gentled into death by those around her.

I arrived at the hospital a half an hour later, and people were quite weary. They went to lunch, and I had the privilege of sitting with Jessica's body for some time. Her face was beautiful. Her right eye was closed, as though she were gazing inward serenely. From the side, she looked like she was in meditation. She did not appear to be dead or even asleep. It was as though an inner awakening had happened. Her left eye was open and gazing up into space. Her mouth was slightly open, as though she had just said, "Ah."

Sitting with that body, I kept asking, "Where did she go? Where has Jessica gone?" I could not imagine that the laughter that I had known just a few days before was not present in some way. I stayed with that question and then did some meditation practices intended for people who have just died.

In a short time the gurney came, and she was lifted into a white plastic bag that was zipped closed. She was taken down the hall by her friends, family, nurses, and the patient advocate. Everyone was very calm, very peaceful. She was put into a station wagon and driven to El Rito, an hour's drive from the hospital.

Jessica had wanted a home burial and had asked to be wrapped in an Indian blanket and put in the coffin that she had designed. The next day her four elder brothers stepped into the grave hole in a snowy field and received her coffin as though they were receiving her back into the earth. Then we began to fill in the gaping hole in the wintry terrain. It took a lot of work to fill up that hole. In the process, I watched grief transform into community.

Issan

Issan Dorsey began to practice Buddhism in the 1960s. His non-Buddhist name was Tommy Dorsey, though he was not the famous musician. Issan founded the Hartford Street Zen Center and the Maitri Hospice in the gay district of San Francisco. At the time he founded Hartford Street, he had not been tested for AIDS. Issan lived in the midst of suffering and death, and he felt it was important to help his brothers who were dying all around him. The hospice and Zen center had a very little physical roof, but Issan was a big roof Buddhist; everything and everybody could fit under the roof of his spirit.

Over the years, Issan and I led several retreats together; and he invited me to be on the board of the hospice. Through Issan and the hospice, I saw how Buddhism could function in a very practical way in a community in crisis. I was also inspired by a Buddhism that was not Buddhist at all. Thich Nhat Hanh has said Buddhism is made of non-Buddhist elements. At the hospice and the Hartford Street Zen Center, you did not feel piety. There was nothing sectarian about this place. You just took refuge under a big roof with others who needed refuge.

We all hoped that Issan would live a long time, but he had only a few more years inside of him. Near the end of his life, he received transmission as a Zen teacher. His mind and the Buddha's mind were recognized as one.

At the time of his transmission ceremony, he could barely walk to the altar. He did not go in traditional robes, but wore a bathrobe and went down to the basement of the hospice, where the *zendo* was located. He was given a chair to sit in, and then he very feebly got up, and Richard Baker Roshi, who gave him transmission, met him halfway. Issan had come a long way, from one point of view, and from another, he was just who he was. He had never left home at all.

One could say that Issan Dorsey had received transmission many times, not just from one teacher to another in a formal way, but from every person he had met. He was not impeded by concepts. He did not carry the load and the burden that most of us do. An assistant of mine, a Zen nun, once said, "I'm listening to a lecture by Issan. Just the most extraordinary lecture I've ever heard, Joan. Not one concept!" We loved Issan for that. It was a great relief to be in his presence. He was a man free of knowledge, a man of wisdom.

After Issan formally became a *roshi,* his health declined further and he was hospitalized. One day I came up from southern California to visit him in the hospital. I have loved deeply many of the dying people with whom I have sat; I have accepted their suffering and deaths with some degree of equanimity. But watching Issan die was hard for me. He had been there for so many, and I wanted him to continue to be there and do the work that had touched all of us. His life taught us all what it meant to be not just a Buddhist, but a true human being, and to be present for another being in such a way that self and other disappear.

One afternoon, I walked into Issan's hospital room. Dressed in a simple cotton Japanese robe, he was sitting up in bed. He was quite thin and transparent. I sat on the side of the bed and looked into his eyes. Suddenly my face was wet. Issan picked up his frail hand and reached over to touch my hand. He looked at me and said, "Please don't cry," and he smiled. I had to return the smile.

In that gesture of kindness, I understood something that I never had before. I thought that I had come there as a caregiver, but in fact Issan was the real bodhisattva. He had held up a mirror that allowed me to see my pity, which was less than necessary; and also the truth of our friendship, which was beyond pity, beyond language, beyond life. I had to let go of Issan.

Issan evoked in me a compassion that was spontaneous. Suddenly the nectar of *bodhicitta* began to flow in my heart. Something subtle connected the two of us, and a line from Rilke came to me at that moment: "Love and death are the great gifts that are given to us. Mostly they are passed on unopened."

I realized in that moment of communion with Issan that we had actually opened the treasure box of love and death. It is said that bodhisattvas, because there are no obstacles for their minds, overcome fear and liberate themselves forever from illusion. In that quality of unconditional relatedness, obstacles disappear. One does not realize this outside the presence of a vowing relationship, a relationship informed by practice and intentionality, a relationship based on the bodhisattva ideal. This is where God appears—not with an individual, but between beings.

Issan once told me a story. In the early 1980s, when the movement against the nuclear arms race was surging, a teacher at the San Francisco Zen Center gave a lecture and repeated the phrase "Everything is OK." Someone in the audience asked, "Roshi, do you still say everything is OK when your country is about to go to war?" Roshi said, "Gee, that's a tough question." The person who asked the question wrote a poem later:

Everything,
just as it is.
As it is.
As is.
Flowers in bloom,
nothing to add,
nothing to reduce.
The entire world,
Hiroshima.

The entire world, Hiroshima. I could look into Issan's face and see Hiroshima. I looked into Jessica's face, and there was Hiroshima. The entire world, Hiroshima. One great catastrophe, one limitless wound. And yet, and yet....

•

People sometimes ask me if it is difficult to be around dying and death. Someone once asked, "How could you touch someone whose body is covered with lesions?" In the beginning, it wasn't easy. I was scared. I felt as if I would get what they had. Breast cancer, colon cancer, uterine cancer, AIDS. One day, I realized that I already had what they had. I was not separate from this one with cancer, that one with AIDS. How could I be afraid of getting what I already had?

Being with people who are suffering can teach us that we are not separate from them. Whatever illness and suffering they are enduring we are also experiencing, even though it may not be directly afflicting our body. We have entered into a covenant with each person who becomes visible to us. Even more than that, as this practice continues, we realize that we are not separate from the suffering of the people in Bosnia or in the rain forests of Kalimantan, Brazil, and southern Mexico. All beings are part of us. When the forests are cut down and a people's ways are diminished, when their cultures are ended, we are impoverished.

In this practice of engaged spirituality, we try to cultivate a very open heart, a heart that opens endlessly. But most of us find it difficult to sustain an undefended heart.

It is grace when the alchemy is there, and both you and the dying person feel that you are on the journey together. But sometimes the dying individual will reject you. I was rejected by a friend with AIDS-related lymphoma. This friend took my hand, held it for a while, pushed it away, and then peacefully headed straight down the highway of death. At first, I felt rejected. I had to smile at my response because my friend was doing just the right thing in letting go of me and others who had gotten close.

It is difficult for many of us to let go of those things and beings that we love. Are we not reminded of this every day of our lives? Can we even let go of our outbreath? We are of the nature to get sick, grow old, and die. We and the amaryllis flower are of the same nature. Where is our compost heap? As Thich Nhat Hanh has reminded us, the rose is in the compost, and the compost is in the rose.

Years ago, I went to St. Simon Island off the coast of Georgia to visit my friend Bessie Jones. She took me to her church, where her son was preaching at a funeral. The old white clapboard building had weathered many storms. She and I joined others sitting on church benches. After the opening hymn, Bessie's son looked into the coffin and then at the congregation and said, "What you see there in the coffin is not what you loved."

•

The bodhisattva has many characteristics. One image of a bodhisattva is the iron man. It refers to the qualities of strength and durability, an iron spine that upholds itself in the midst of all conditions. Here can be no attachment to outcome: good death, bad death, not important. Death is inevitable. How you do it is your story. This is the way of the iron man—a pivot of intention to be fully present in this moment, an intention that is so fierce that nothing can move it. This is in your true spine.

In being with dying and in being with living, you gather up your nervous system, plant it in your spine, and feel the iron strength within you. You are present for whatever happens.

Another image of the bodhisattva is a wooden puppet. This puppet is simply responding to the world. It has no personal desire or agenda. If somebody is hungry, give him food. If somebody is sleepy, help her find a bed. When somebody needs a sponge bath, give him a sponge bath. No big deal; just respond to things exactly as they are.

Twenty years ago, a friend of mine named Susanna Valadez went to the Huichol country as a young anthropologist. After she had been in a particular village a short time, a family arrived. The mother was carrying an infant who looked quite neglected, as if it was going to die very shortly. Susanna asked, "What are you doing with the baby?" The mother and father said, "Well, the baby is going to die." Susanna said, "Give me the baby." She took the baby and washed it, fed it, put it in her bed, and slept that night with it. When she awakened in the morning, the baby was dead. The Huichols, being Huichols, laughed and said, "See, we told you the baby was going to die." Susanna told me, "If I had it to do all over again, I would do the same thing."

A spiritual life is not about self-consciousness or wearing a button that says you are a Buddha or bodhisattva. It is doing what you have to do, without any attachment to outcome. When I sit with a dying person whose body is covered with lesions, I breathe with him. I know that the outcome for that person, like the outcome for each one of us, is the same.

Regardless of outcome, you do the best you can. You do it simply because it is the right thing to do, and you cannot look to the outcome. You respond like the wooden puppet to suffering, offering love and compassion without any conditions. You uphold yourself in strength and openness, like the iron man. You have no gaining idea, no attachment to outcome. You do this with choiceless awareness. As Yasutani Roshi once said, "The compassion of the undifferentiated body of no-cause comes burning forth."

Practicing in the World

Many people think of Buddhism as a self-involved practice of sitting on a cushion, staring at one's navel, and not doing other people much good. But meditation practice can help cultivate stability, deepheartedness, and openness, making it possible for one to be with suffering.

Engaged Buddhism is about being with forests that are dying, oceans that are polluted, hearts that are in pain, and children who have been sexually abused. Engaged Buddhism expresses itself in both great and small ways. In this practice of engaged Buddhism, whatever form of suffering we are working with, whether it is on a global scale or the most intimate scale of being there for a family member, we are learning about compassion. We are on our knees.

Bernie Glassman is a Buddhist who helps give shelter to the homeless. He sits in the rubble and finds gold. His work reminds us that we all need refuge and that we can take our practice and our altars into the street.

Bill Devall is an environmentalist, a deep ecologist, and an activist. He is not just a philosopher. He puts his altar in the redwoods and his body on the line.

Joanna Macy is a peaceful warrior, speaking out about human rights violations in Tibet, nuclear waste, and environmental problems all over the world. Joanna, heart open, asks people to touch their own suffering and despair. Her altar is a nuclear dump site.

And Sister Chan Khong, Sister True Emptiness, is a Vietnamese nun working for the freedom of incarcerated Vietnamese monks and teachers. The veins of her heart are strong and touch many. Her altar is her breath.

Engaged Buddhism is practiced by these precious people, but it is also practiced by many people whom we will never know, individuals whose lives are completely ordinary and whose acts will go unsung. When I was in Vietnam some years ago, I met men and women in the School of Youth for Social Service. They had been young people during the war; now their hair was gray and there were lines around their eyes. Even after Thây had been gone from their country for nearly thirty years, they were still helping flood victims, working in orphanages, helping people with leprosy, and carrying the light of compassion forward in the world.

They are humble people whose names I cannot now remember, but I saw the purity of mind and heart in their gaze and true selflessness in what they did. In their everyday lives, they do not try to inspire us in a big way, but rather they do many small acts of kindness with a natural compassion that makes it possible for the world to shine a little more.

George Eliot ends *Middlemarch* with the following words: "The growing good of the world is partly dependent on unhistoric acts; and that things are not so ill with you and me as they might have been, is half owing to the number who lived faithfully a hidden life, and rest in unvisited tombs."

Taking Refuge

The Buddha did not awaken because he relied on the Sutras. Some of us think that we can wake up because of the Bible or the Sutras, but they can also be an obstacle. It might be said that the Buddha woke up because he had abandoned the Sutras. For many of us, going on means going far. It means we leave the familiar, the habitual home ground. Yet, as it is said in the *Tao Te Ching,* going far means returning, finding what our true home and our true nature are, taking refuge in big mind, big sky. Abandoning the life that seemed right for us may return us to our true home. Here we find the sutra of the ordinary, the sutra of the everyday.

My own life has been a sutra on leaving home and returning. I left all kinds of homes and went through the kind of loneliness that people experience when they step off the familiar road, when they step away from a community, when they step away from the habits of comfort, and when they lose their minds. It is deep loneliness, but one that teaches us how to give. It can awaken within us natural generosity. Many of us turn away from this loneliness. It can feel so unbearable. Can we bear this loneliness? Can we discover the treasure of generosity in solitude?

•

When I formally took refuge in Buddhism in 1976, in the so-called Three Jewels, I thought I was taking refuge in the historical Buddha, in the doctrine known as the *dharma,* and in the Buddhist community known as the *sangha.* Twenty years later, I see things quite differently. I now see through the heart that longs for others to be free.

I see that what we really take refuge in is not only the historical Buddha, but each being's gift for awakening. If we have faith in that, the possibility of being free from suffering is much greater. When I look into the eyes of those who are dying, I see both life and death clearly written. I also see freedom from life and death. I recognize that I am taking refuge, not in life and not in death, but in the space between life and death. It is not a Buddhist, Christian, or Jew who is dying. A Buddha is dying. A Buddha is going home.

When I now take refuge in the *dharma,* I understand that I am not simply taking refuge in the doctrine of a very intelligent and gifted Asian man who taught twenty-five hundred years ago, or in books about the philosophy and psychology of the tradition that grew up through and around him. Rather, I am taking refuge in the truth that one discovers in mindful noticing.

I am taking refuge in a truth that is deeper than concepts, dogma, and ideology. I am taking refuge in the eyes of love, in the undivided ground of being. I take refuge in the interdependence of the relative and the absolute. Things exist as a result of conditions, causes, and relatedness; and nothing exists in the absolute sense in terms of any unchanging, permanent reality or identity.

When I take refuge in the *sangha,* I am not only taking refuge in a particular Buddhist group, but also in the greater community. If we look deeply, we can see that everything is practicing with us. The trees, the clouds, each person we meet is part of our *sangha.* I cherish my local *sangha.* And I know that the rain that is falling as I write these words is my *sangha,* too. Even our enemies practice with us, teaching us unconditional love and compassion.

But what does refuge point to? What does it mean to come home, to be free from suffering, to be sheltered by a big and open sky? Thich Nhat Hanh once said that "the moment of awakening is marked by an outburst of laughter. But this is not the laughter of someone who suddenly acquires a great fortune. Neither is it the laughter of one who has won a great victory. It is, rather, the laughter of one who after having painfully searched for something a very long time finds it one morning in the pocket of his coat." This freedom is here within us at this very moment. Freedom then reveals the love that is also present and possible with our lives and between us.

Lama Lodro Dorje once wrote, "Issues of love bear on our opening to the basic nature of reality as compassion and on beginning to see that we are fundamentally not separate from others or from the basic ground. This makes our ability to love and our nourishment from love more unconditional. Love is not merely an emotion. It is a meltdown that reestablishes a more unified space of brilliance, goodness, and sadness. This is the function of love in spiritual tradition."

Spirituality is difficult for us to touch because it flows to and from the invisible, from love and the mystery of death. It comes out of the "meltdown" that we know as love and compassion and the surrender that we know as death. It flows from the ground of our relationship, not only between human beings, but also between all beings, including mountains and rivers. It is often born from suffering, and it evokes within us compassion, which allows us to see through the eyes of innumerable beings.

My friend Kazuaki Tanahashi and I often say that we are Zen failures. People are usually more interested in victories than in struggles; but in a Buddhist way, we see that a spiritual life frequently opens through a door of suffering. Suffering and failure bring us to practice and teach us about our strengths and our interconnectedness with all beings. Our failures can transform into understanding and compassion.

It seems appropriate to close with a poem by Antonio Machado:

Last night I had a dream.
Oh wonderful error!
I dreamt that here in my heart,
golden bees were making honey
and white combs
out of my old forgotten failures.

I bow to the bees and honey and to all our old forgotten failures.